Network Marketing Survival

"Choosing the Right Company & Always Making Profit From Them All!"

**from the Library of the
New Thrive Learning Institute**

Published 2016 under Creative Commons License -
NonCommercial-ShareAlike 3.0 Unported

Get Related Materials

from Our Free Library

Instant Access – Join Here

Click or type into your browser:

http://livesensical.com/go/byob/

LEGAL NOTICE

Table of Contents

The Shocking Truth!

If you are reading this book, let me first congratulate you if you are a newcomer to the world of MLM and allowing me to impart my experiences on the industry to help you in taking the first step into this fantastic industry.

My intentions of writing this book is to help and provide people generic information that would apply to any company regardless on their marketing/compensation plan, product, team, country or even offline or online!

It is indeed a shocking truth to find out that over 95% of network marketers or home based business owners are operating their business at a LOSS!

How scary if you are reading this for the first time.

Well thankfully if we all worshiped statistics fanatically, most people today will be afraid to drive cars or even go to school (e.g. the percentage of road accidents and how many students in a class 'make it' in getting distinctions)

We all want to be smart people and rather be in the top 5% being the ones making the money now, don't we? Of course we do.

It is sad that countless of poor victims join the industry, uninformed, and when they run into problems, they usually put the blame on the company, the team or even the industry itself!

That is why we hope to avoid such unfortunate circumstances.

Even if you have been involved, this information is invaluable because it might teach you things you have missed out or information to help your downline. So, let's proceed...

Why Would You Be Choosing an MLM in The First Place

MLM survival. Let's face it, the world out there is like a jungle. More particularly so in the MLM world. It would be easy to say, since it is that difficult, let's just forget about the whole MLM or network marketing deal in the first place (then this book would not be necessary at all). That action would be self-defeating.

There is good news for all of us. So let us instead start from a positive note.

The purpose of this book is not just about teaching you to choose the right MLM Company but also how, by being properly educated about the industry, you will be able to receive benefits from every opportunity you invest your time and money in. The information here will be completely generic and neutral. I am not endorsing any company over the other as there is no such thing as the perfect MLM but rather choosing an MLM that is SUITABLE for YOU!

Whatever your reasons may be, let us make a few assumptions about it before we proceed (or else you wouldn't pay for this E-book in the first place)

- Making money
- Saving money on products
- Meeting new people
- Growth and development

Making Money
- Looking for fast money

- Building a long term business with money coming in long after you have 'retired'
- Investing in the product itself

For people looking for fast money, there are pros and cons to this kind of thinking.

Some people are WELL TRAINED salesmen. They have built the relationship with their clients, customers and all sorts of people. People trust what they say and will trust whatever they are selling. They may sell the product itself (sometimes, in large quantities), or they may sell the opportunity (the money making part of it) or both. Are YOU this kind of person?

Fast money is not impossible, but it COULD be for the short term only. Consider the facts that 80-90% of people in the world are NOT built for sales. If a salesman sponsors a non-salesman, would the non-salesman be able to do the same thing as his upline? Does that mean that I would spend most of my time looking for the 10-20% of sales types?

The next type of money is the long term type.

When I define long term, it does not have to mean that you might not see money right away. It differs from company to company. But as a general rule of thumb, it involves BUILDING A NETWORK OR AN ORGANISATION.

The key to building a large organization as quoted by Zig Ziglar, *"You will get whatever you want in life if you will just help enough other people get what they want."* In other words, if you will help enough downlines get enough downlines, you are on the road to network marketing financial freedom. The key is to help others.

There is one more category of people who 'invests' in network marketing companies, not to make money through retaining or networking, but rather investing in the product, position, or depending on the company, appreciation of their 'assets'. A few examples would be investing in a product, so that in the future, its value will appreciate, so you can sell it to other people at a very high margin (sort of like old comic books.) Others might purchase the account or distributorship from you (depending on the compensation plan of the company) while some Internet companies actually pay you to 'invest' in their company, sort of like buying a share of the company.

Saving Money on Products

Retailing of a product is very important to an MLM business. Lack of (or even non-existing) retailing could be harmful to the distributor or the company as certain states have outlawed 'headhunting' and have their own policies.

Nevertheless, saving money on an MLM product is one of the most wonderful key features of joining an MLM company if recruiting is not your forte.

In certain compensation plans, repeat purchase of the products you buy from the company gives you more rebates or bonuses. In essence, the more you buy, the cheaper it becomes. This becomes an even greater pleasure if you are totally in love with the products or you have already set aside a budget for those products (which means you are now buying from the MLM company or your upline instead of buying from the supermarket, pharmacy, grocery store, etc)

There are some important aspects to take note however, if the company requires you to purchase the products in bulk (hence the term – frontloading), is there a DEMOTION in your achieved position in the company, is there MAINTAINANCE required, or how much are the renewal fees for membership. All these will be further discussed in the later chapters.

Meeting New People

This is one of the many reasons why people join MLM companies (even if the first two reasons discussed above don't even concern them). There are all types of people in the world. Some like the positive environment. Others like the social events the company or team organizes. Some look for a potential life partner there!

Lots of people even go all out to join these kind of businesses to get more contacts for their OWN BUSINESSES (maybe even THEIR OWN MLM BUSINESS). Bear in mind one thing. There is this old saying that goes, you scratch my back, I scratch yours. If you participate in their activities but don't go full force in their company/team vision, don't expect them to join you or buy from you. There may even be negative repercussions (such as being banned from coming back to the company).

Growth and Development

One of the biggest reasons why I would recommend joining an MLM company and doing the business is opening your mind to positive thinking and achieving your full potential. There are many companies out there who have the best training courses, motivational rallies, sharing sessions and whopping transformation camps that will not only fire you up but take your business building to the next level.

I will not touch much on this subject extensively here. There are so many companies out there that will do a fantastic job in terms of training.

Remember that growth is a journey and not a destination.

Types of People Who Are Looking For Opportunities

Remember that people join MLM companies for their own reasons. However, the character or intention of a person will determine how far they want to go in MLM. Here are classic examples of different types of people

- Genuine business opportunity seekers and builders
- Product consumers
- The supporters
- MLM junkies
- 001 syndrome

Genuine business opportunity seekers are the most important people in building a large business. They are the bread and butter. Not all are leaders but leaders are not born, they are developed. This group of people also can be product consumers.

Product consumers are people who join an MLM and buy from them because they like the product and enjoy the service of their upline. They are not necessarily genuine business opportunity seekers or builders yet for many builders, a lot of their income will come from this group. The good thing about them is as they learn more about the product, the company and interact more with their upline, their exposure to MLM grows and they might convert to opportunity seekers and then builders.

The supporters' category is quite a mixed match of people. When their close friends or relatives build an MLM, they will join under them to 'support their businesses. However, the consequence of that action varies according to the individual. For example, I would join my friend's organization but it could be purely out of obligation and not for any genuine reason. This could potentially lead to resentment (when you mix business dealings with friendship), confusion and even loss of friends. Others might even join to see if their friend or relative is involved in a scam to try and pull him or her out. In order to prevent any potential disaster, make sure your intentions for joining an MLM are very clear cut.

MLM junkies are the sort of people who jump from MLM to MLM (some people even call them Multi-Level-Monkeys). They attend a talk, get hyped up about the opportunity, and build the business on euphoria. Sooner or later, they lose steam and find problems with the company (when the real problem is themselves most of the time) and jump to the next SMOKING HOT business opportunity. It is not wrong to be a member of many MLM companies (depending on your budget). Bear in mind, certain companies discourage or even forbid you to join other companies (then their business practices should be examined). If you are a member of many companies, it is OK to do a good survey and attend trainings, but the key to remember is you must focus on ONE good MLM for the long run and the others can operate on a referral basis (like recommending a friend to buy a product from another company while building one main one).

This leads us to one more category of people who could be MLM junkies as well – the 001 syndrome. Basically they want to be the first to start building a business in a brand new start-up. They want to be the pioneer. There are many pros and cons to assess about a new company like their background history, financial status and product market rather than just focusing on the income potential. There are many more challenges to be faced for people who are sponsored directly under the company and new companies don't usually have a time-tested workable system in place.

If you fall into one of the above categories (or even some or all of the above), these will give you a general guideline on how to improve your choice selection of MLM companies before we go in to the details about compensation plans and product demand. By knowing yourself better, you can do a better assessment.

What is the MLM Jungle Like

There are thousands of MLM companies out there! Here are a few categories of MLM. These will help you determine which company suits you.

> **Product/Servicing**
>
> **Traditional MLM**
>
> **Concept**
>
> **Physical product**
>
> **Internet MLM**
>
> **Digital Product**

The main difference between traditional MLM and Internet MLM is the method used to recruit or sponsor. Traditional MLM relies mostly on one-on-one prospecting (like at a McDonald's or Starbuck's), home party, opportunity meetings or rallies. Internet MLM does the recruiting through e-mail, newsletter, forums, websites and sales letters. This minimizes the human interaction part and may be more suitable for those who are not very good at talking to others.

Two main types of traditional MLM are one that is heavily concerned with retailing, consumption or distribution of a physical product. Typically one with a high volume of repeat sale (like vitamins or skin care products) and good testimonials of the product with high visibility (e.g. look at my skin, the product has cured all my pimples!).

Concept MLM doesn't focus as much on products compared to its former counterpart. They usually do have a product, but it doesn't have as high a repeat sale as those mentioned above. Most of them run their business like a club. Some are like lifestyle clubs. Others conduct their business with a high degree of professionalism (they all dress better than an office worker). Often they will sell their people a dream or molding them to a particular image to convey the image of the company for attracting more recruits. It's the sizzle that sells the steak.

In Internet MLM, there are distributions of two types of products. A physical product distributed through the Internet means that the Internet does the selling and recruiting, taking the orders, and the shipment of the product are done offline. Digital products remove the headaches of physical product distribution. This usually gives the company a better margin due to lower overheads (no warehousing or shipment).

Exposure to the Industry

In the MLM industry, there are a few factors to consider when considering which company to build a long term business.

Product background

Marketing or Compensation plan

The team (Upline, Sidelines, even the company staff)

The trend of the time

First off: It has been said in the past – your UPLINE chooses the first company you join. It still is the case today for many who are either unexposed and their friends or relatives who join an MLM first approaches them.

The unexposed might oblige their upline and if they are not careful, will cause a very bad first impression on the industry.

Today, you don't need to be picked by someone else. You can choose first. Do a good survey based on the guidelines above. As a matter of fact, you don't even need to join the first person who invited you in a company. You have a choice to choose someone else to be your upline within the SAME company.

Products are very crucial in MLM. Just because one company says our product is the 'best' doesn't mean that it is. Just like any other business, people seriously building an MLM will only say good things about their own product. They will even give fantastic and even outrageous testimonials about how the product can help them.

Many are very sincere and well-meaning, but the rule of thumb to remember is – yes, you say the product is the best, but that is also because you haven't tried any others because you are in this business!

I firmly believe that most MLM products are of exceptional quality. That is because the product must work then only can the distributor give good testimonials due to the nature of the distributor doing direct sales (dealing directly with the prospect/customer). There are companies that DISCOURAGE their people from using products from a competitor MLM (some even ask you to stop buying from the supermarket and buy from your 'own business' instead).

Beware: some even go as far as to talk down about the products of other MLM companies. Most people, in their zealous zeal to recruit others, may use this tactic. This is often perceived as rather unprofessional.

Bear in mind: in MLM, if you talk bad about other MLM companies or their products, you are talking bad about the entire industry as a WHOLE (you mean to say that only your company, product, compensation plan, team is the best in the world and the rest of all the other companies are of inferior quality? Man... I don't want to be in this industry.) Can you imagine if every network marketer is doing this? No wonder the industry has a bad name!

The Marketing or Compensation Plan

The plan is very important. It shows how much work you need to do to get paid this much. All marketing plans have their own advantages and disadvantages. Different companies offer different margins for their products. The key to remember in margin comparison, if the company pays the distributor too low, you might not survive; if the margin is too exorbitantly high, you might earn a lot, but your retail customers will suffer and the business might not be long term.

Before I share with you a few more popular type of marketing plan to give you an idea about what company will offer what, I wish to highlight two things in every plan: DEMOTION and MAINTAINANCE

DEMOTION means dropping from one MLM position to a lower one (usually resulting in a loss of future potential income) or your remainder quota required to reach a certain target is increased (the volume achieved in the past do now count towards the grand total anymore) Demotion is an important factor to consider in every marketing plan as someone who suffers demotion suffers a sudden loss in income and could be very embarrassing to others.

MAINTENANCE (sometimes called auto-ship) is the minimum amount of sales volume (usually every month) a distributor or serious business builder has to buy either his own personal volume or combined with group sales in order to maintain his rank, be eligible for bonuses, overriding commission or sometimes even maintain his distributorship. Having maintenance or no maintenance all has its pros and cons. I will highlight 3 scenarios to give a clearer picture.

A) MANDATORY MAINTENANCE

Some companies require you to purchase products every single month. This is good if you have built a large organization and it ensures you have guaranteed income every month. Not good if you are forced to maintain and you are not making money in your business. If you are in love with the product and don't mind paying for it every month then it is fine. But this can cause a person who is not seriously building or is still struggling with his business some pressure and it is one of the main causes of drop out in MLM.

If the maintenance is too expensive, people might shun the company. However, the upline with a lot of people in his group can build a large stable income this way. Some companies may not require you to maintain at the early stages and increases the maintenance after they achieve a certain rank.

B) NO MAINTENANCE

This is very good for people who have just started their business or for people who is just casually 'trying out' an MLM. There is no pressure and a person can be in an MLM for years but still at the same rank.

The bad news is that it might not be good for the long term (because no maintenance means no downlines need to buy anything) unless your group is in love with the product or if you and your downlines have built a solid customer base and the demand of the product it there.

C) OPTIONAL MAINTENANCE

This is also very good for people who just started or the casual type. They will only ask you to buy a certain volume of products when you want to override your commission from the company. This is also very good in the sense that you are not pressured to pay maintenance and you only pay when you are making money.

There is one problem with this, however. Among the serious business builders if the downlines are not producing any sales, even having a large organization will not pay you well if not at all (just like a zero maintenance company, no downline sales means those in the middle will not maintain, causing a chain reaction all the way to the uplines at the top). This is a hollow organization where your rank/title means nothing without income.

Types of Plans

Next, I will go in detail about the more popular types of plans...

1) The Stairstep
2) The Unilevel
3) The Binary
4) The Breakaway
5) The Matrix
6) The Australian Two Up
7) The Hybrid

1) The Stairstep

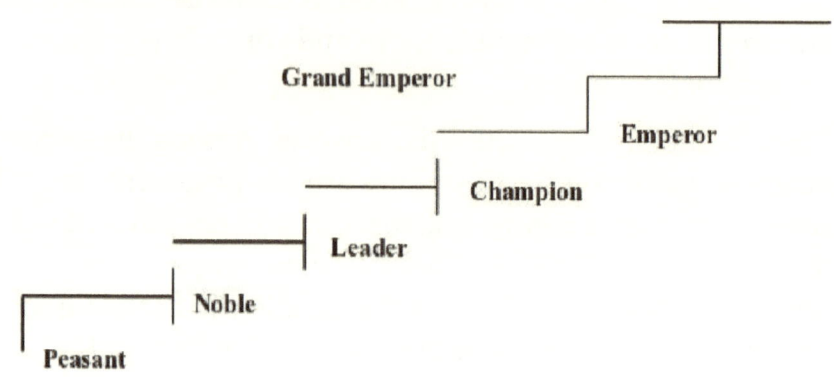

The Stairstep or step and ladder plan is a simple plan that has requirements that you must meet to get up the "Stairs of Success" Every step is a promotion usually based on achieving a certain volume and each promotion or rank gives you a larger cut.

Demotion in stairstep plans to ensure a distributor's group commits to a certain volume every month. It gives a particular rank a guaranteed income. Demotion in this case means that you must either maintain a certain volume every month (or quarter or fiscal year) in order to maintain that rank. Let us say for example, Anthony achieves a sales volume of $200,000 in his entire team (for a certain timeframe) and that promotes him from Leader to Champion, certain companies require him to keep up that same sales volume the next time or else he will be demoted back to a leader. In certain plans, there is no demotion in rank, so the group sales are accumulated for reaching the next level.

Maintenance here plays a key factor how building a solid group will look like. If there are low repeat sales for the product being marketed, expect the minimum entry fee to be higher than the average MLM. This is because low repeat sales means less maintenance hence the majority of the income comes from recruiting new blood. If nobody does maintenance in a Stairstep plan, having a high rank doesn't earn you money so don't be a fool if someone tells you that the 'minimum' income for a 'grand emperor' is $100,000 a month – it all depends on the volume generated. On the contrary, plans with maintenance involved do guarantee an income or else you will not be in that rank.

This type of plan is one of the oldest and longest plans around. The advantage of climbing the ladder gives major incentives for distributors to work harder and fight for the target. The larger your group the more you override even up to infinity levels as long as your downline is of a lower rank than you. There is also a fair system involved lets say if your downline works harder than you and sponsors more people, he can actually have a rank higher than you and that is when breakaway in certain plans come into play (discussed in the breakaway plan below)

The disadvantage however, is once a downline reaches a certain rank (lets say you need 3 directly sponsored leaders to qualify as a champion), one of them becomes a leader while you focus on making the remaining 2 groups to become leaders, the first leader might be neglected in the process. The other disadvantage is if the downline is too far deep in the organization (lets say your downline's downline all the way down 10 generations), some distributors may neglect helping them because the monetary incentive is too small.

2) The Unilevel

The Unilevel is a simple "Number of levels" that the company will pay you, and usually there is no promotion or rank. You make money by getting a certain override off of the volume, and usually there is a requirement of volume to qualify for a check.

The advantage here is you don't have work your butt off during certain seasons to fight for that rank. You can sponsor as many people as you can and your income comes from a large volume of people in your organization. For example, you can personally sponsor 5 people, and these 5 will look for 5. after 4 generations you will have 5 to the power of 4 in your organization (780 people) and the calculation of your sales volume will give you a straight forward income.

The disadvantage however, is there is no incentive for developing many different groups (called legs). In spite of conditions in a plan imposed by the company (that you have to sponsor a minimum number of legs) some unilevel people tend to let the 'strong' downlines do all the work as in wait for their downlines to sponsor MORE people than themselves, which is a poor reflection of leadership.

In the Unilevel, there is no demotion (the only demotion is leaving the company) and maintenance plays a key part in the long term income.

3) The Binary

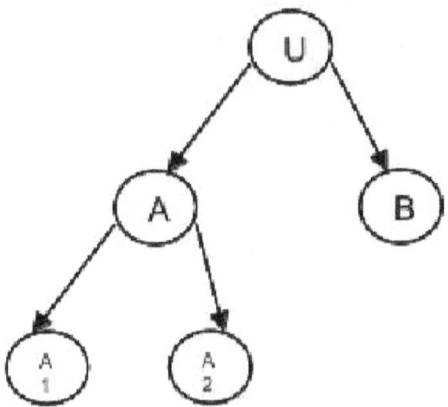

The Binary is an interesting design for a Comp Plan. It usually has 2 "legs" that you can have "Business centers" in, and you have a volume requirement to get paid on each leg. There is what is called "balancing". in the Binary...you must balance the volume from each both A and B group to make sure you maximize your commissions. In the illustration above, the A group is the strong leg (or the giant leg) while the B group is called the weak leg (or the profit leg). A has more people than B (assume they all produce the same volume per person). B needs to find 2 more people in order for U to 'balance' hence maximizing U's income.

The main advantage of this plan is spill over. Allow me to illustrate:

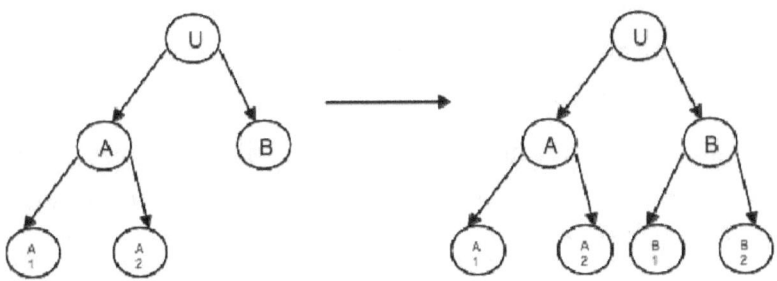

U sponsors 2 friends. In a binary, the company limits each distributor to have a MAXIMUM of 2 people. A and B were previously recruited by U. U needs to 'balance' his group by helping B find 2 people. But let us assume that B is not actively building the business at the moment, so what does U do? He finds and sponsors 2 people HIMSELF and places both of them under B and they become B1 and B2. This is called SPILLOVER.

The advantage of spill over is that when everyone works as a team, the tree will fill very fast as all uplines and downlines work together to balance each other's networks. It is also immune to the problems in unilevel or stairstep plans with downlines being too deep in the organization. A binary can be balance depending on which side the downline is in and not how deep.

The disadvantage however, is that this plan is particularly attractive to lazy people who don't do any work and expect free handouts from their uplines. Imagine what will happen if everyone waits for their upline to place people under them? It doesn't develop strength.

4) The Breakaway

This plan has been said to have become somewhat unpopular in the industry, as you could lose the business you build, once it gets to a certain level of success, and it "breaks away" to no longer be a part of what you get paid on. It usually appears in stairstep. Lets use the example above in the stairstep illustration.

If I am a Champion and my downline builds his organization faster than me, and qualifies as an Emperor before me, 2 things might happen.

Depending on the company's pay structure, I will not be eligible to receive overriding commissions from my downline Emperor's group. Hence the 'breakaway' his bonuses will be 'passed up' to MY upline Emperor or Grand Emperor. In some cases, the ENTIRE group breaks away and join MY upline so even if I do qualify as an Emperor later on, I will not receive bonuses from his group! Selfish people might even involve in SABOTAGE as in trying to slow down his downline from breaking away or overtaking him.

Today, more and more companies are acknowledging the breakaway problem and will start awarding leadership development bonuses (such as a fixed bonus percentage over that entire group even those they have broken away). This system has still worked out well in the past though, because it gets people working harder to prevent the breakaway from happening.

In MLM (just like in life), companies reward PEOPLE who work hard to build their groups. If a downline works harder than his upline, he should get paid more – hence it is more fair to them. So in this case if an upline doesn't work hard enough, he shouldn't blame the company if the downline breaks away.

5) The Matrix

The matrix or sometimes called a FORCED MATRIX is like a pre-order tree. A computer driven plan puts into your group by computer, and they go in the next available slot. Usually this plan is combined with some form of a Binary (sometimes 3 by 9 or 5 by 25 matrix depending on the maximum 'width' allowed), and it does work well if there are a lot of people that are recruited and WORKING TOGETHER TO FILL THE MATRIX. When you recruit someone, the computer searches down for the next open slot, and positions them there. There are some plans that allow you to override the commission of those that you personally sponsor even though they are not positioned directly under you within the tree.

How the computer works is like this:

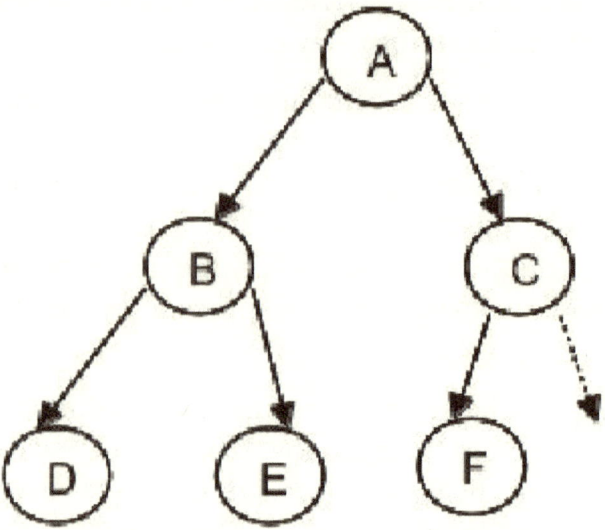

D sponsors a new friend. That new friend doesn't get slotted under D but rather fills the last position which is the dotted line under C. Once they fill up to a certain level, the distributor gets paid a lump sum.

Once again, the advantages here is that every single distributor in the tree all work together to fill the matrix and the duplication result is fantastic! Imagine if everyone finds 2 and everyone does the same thing, the matrix will be filled very fast. This means that even if you don't look for ANYONE to join the company, you will get paid when the tree reaches a certain level.

The biggest and most obvious disadvantage is everybody waiting for everyone to fill the tree thinking that they will get their money waiting for others to fill it. This kind of thinking is EXTREMELY WRONG and will ruin the company. Furthermore, unless there is a cut off system in the marketing plan, (for example, after the sixth level the person at the highest position will have to reinvest again at the bottom of the tree), the guy who 'came first' will get all the commissions and not do anything. By placing a cut off point, everyone who reinvests again will fill the tree faster as the deeper you go down the tree, the more people are needed to fill each level.

6) The Australian Two Up

This is a marketing plan that is very unique. Basically, the two people you recruit are 'given' to your upline sponsor and the rest of the recruits are yours. Here is an illustration:

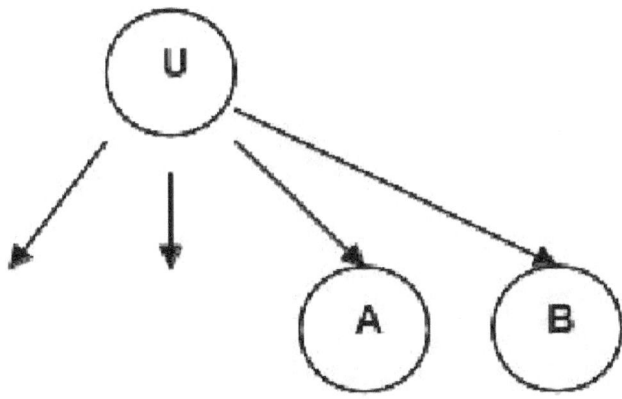

Assume that each person you recruit, you are eligible to earn $100. U sponsors Q1, Q2, A and B. You earn ONLY on A and

B but not on Q1 and Q2 as those sales go to your UPLINE
SPONSOR. Q1 and Q2 are your qualifying sales. Basically by
finding Q1 and Q2, you have basically qualified to earn from
A and B and subsequently C, D, E and as many as you would
like.

Similarly,

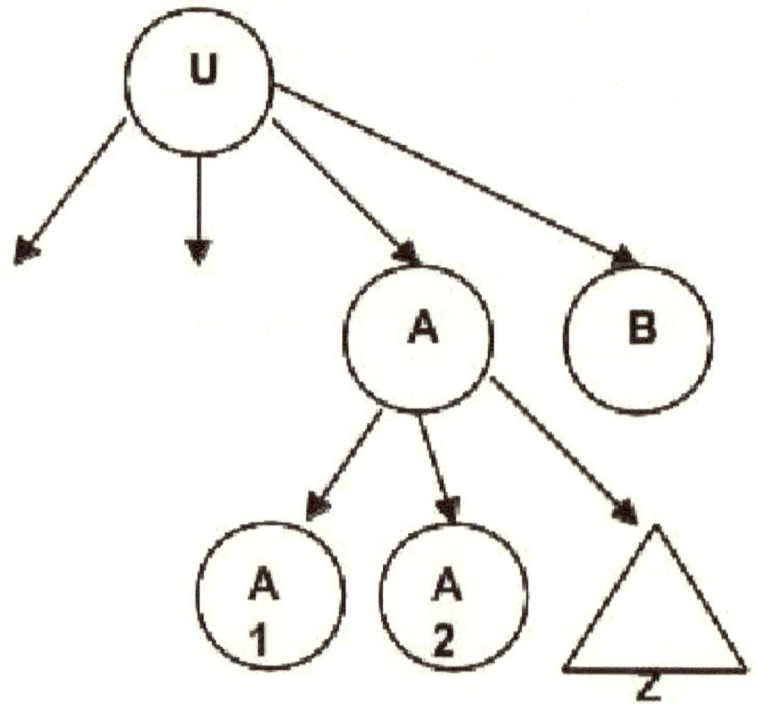

A recruits A1, A2 and Z. The sales of A1 and A2 goes up to U
and the sales of Z goes up to A. As long as U keeps Q1 and Q2
going, he is eligible to earn as wide as he wants and as deep
as he wants! (A1 and A2 is now part of U's group. This will
multiply by 2 each time it goes deeper enabling him to earn
income up to Infinity levels!)

The biggest disadvantage of this plan is that sometimes people are selfish and will only leave U with 'weak' distributors (for example, Q1 and Q2 are slow learners) while capitalizing on the stronger ones in A and B (leaving the strong ones for themselves). Some might even purchase dummy accounts (known as 'cats and dogs' or 'potatoes') This leaves their upline with non-moving legs and creates a hollow organization. Some companies deal with this problem by giving bonuses or special overriding mechanisms where you get special bonuses for building them, or even removing the 'qualified' status should Q1 or Q2 drops out.

7) The Hybrid

A hybrid is a combination of any of the above features. An example would be a Forced Matrix with Unilevel benefits (ensuring that those who actually WORK to fill the tree gets paid more), or an Australian Two Up with Stairstep advancement (to offset the disadvantages of distributors being too deep in an organization)

Many companies that are combining the advantages of many plans to help distributors maximize their income.

Reality check: regardless of how good any plan may sound, none of these plans will make you money if you don't sponsor anyone and develop them.

Only YOU can make the plan work for without you, the plan is dead.

DO NOT get too complicated about Compensation plans. Keep it simple while explaining to your prospects and make sure you understand that you CAN MAKE MONEY with it if you work your plan.

The 3 General Areas to make money in any MLM plan.

1) The First area is Retail Profit.

You must show the prospect that they can earn a retail profit with your products and services. The margin can be anything from 10% to 50%.

2) The Second Area is Team Overrides.

This is where, just like a Real Estate broker, or Insurance agency, you get to develop your own sales team. 'Sales Managers' get paid a certain % of override off of them, just like the Real Estate and Insurance Agents do. Your goal is to help your people do the same thing. People don't understand that you have to help people or help your team in order to succeed. If they achieve success first, then only you will succeed.

3) The Third Area is Leadership Bonuses.

This is where you help develop Successful leaders in your group, and you get an additional bonus or override form your group. You get rewarded by helping others develop their leadership potential. Once your leaders are in place, your MLM business will go on autopilot.

The Team (Upline, Sidelines, even the Company Staff)

Joining the right team is also crucial in MLM. No man is an island in this world. Uplines will always be there to help but the attitude to be adopted is that I am in business for myself but not by myself. Since I am in business for myself, I am the master of my fate, I create my own luck, and I am the author of my own book – it all boils down to ME. Having an upline to help you is considered a BONUS. If you were to run a traditional business, would you expect other people to open shop for you and close the shop for you? Same goes in MLM.

Like wise, you have to be a good, responsible upline as well. No one has succeeded in any industry without learning and MLM is no different. It is the upline's responsibility to guide, train, teach and motivate the downline. New people in MLM without guidance are like sheep wandering into a wild forest – what are their chances of survival? It is no wonder 95% of Network Marketers fail to break even. The upline must lead them, empower them but must never spoon feed them. Uplines must not be abused. **If you give a man a fish, he will feed himself for a day. Teach him to fish, and he will feed himself for life!**

Sidelines or Crosslines are people not in your line of sponsorship. Why should I bother with sidelines? They are all somebody's downline. Somewhere 'up' the line they are probably in one of your upline's group. Many companies now encourage sideline team support. Because you will always have more sidelines than uplines and downlines, it is crucial that side lines help one another. One upline has limited time and resources, but if sidelines work as a team, you leverage on more people.

Developing a good relationship with the company staff is also necessary for success. Imagine if you are holding a team meeting and you need them to arrange or prepare the rooms for you. Getting shipment on time for your products? Check with the staff. If you have a good relationship with the owners of the company, it is also a great advantage for moving in the same direction together. This is even more so for pioneers with a new company, the first batch of distributors and the owners of the company must work closely together to bring the company to success.

The Trend of the Time

One last aspect to consider about a company is the state of it's current market trend. Many people at one time or another has heard about aggressive marketing and campaigns on certain companies based on the need for their product and how hot the opportunity is at the moment.

They could be in the pioneer stage, marketing the latest health products to a growing or maturing market (for example, aging baby boomers). Some could be in a mature stage after surviving in the market over 10 years.

The comparison of the new, smoking hot companies over the mature, or aging counterparts have its pros and cons. New companies are not vulnerable to saturation. Collaboration with new companies put you in positions of power where you can negotiate with the management team on the direction of the company or even enhance the marketing plan. People who has heard of those new companies may jump on the opportunity and it is generally easier to create a large group in a short time.

This does not mean you should not join older companies. Older companies are more stable and has survived the times. They have run a time tested system which has helped many people to succeed. International companies are even more reliable as they have the manpower to tap the international market. Think of McDonald's. They have been around for so many decades yet people are still profiting from them today because they all follow a system.

There is No Such Thing as a Perfect MLM

In spite of all there is discussed above, certain companies may claim they are the best. Different companies market different products and they all claim to be the best in their line. Each claim to be selling the best skin care, nutrition, aromatherapy, insurance programs, investment opportunities or even online digital products.

Let's face it. There is no such thing as a perfect MLM, just there is no such thing as a perfect church or perfect government. MLM companies are just like normal companies in the sense that there will always be management problems, staff problems, cash flow problems, shipment difficulties and product faults.

Take the skin care industry for example. There are many skin care products that have long histories, extensive research, powerful testimonials, and so on. But no matter how good the skin care is, they will not benefit EVERY SINGLE PERSON ON THE PLANET. We are all different. Some has drier skin. Some are more sensitive. You can't prescribe a drug that will cure everything for everyone.

Likewise with teams. Certain teams are more suitable for younger crowds with all the excitement and the hoo-hah going on. Others are for a more mature crowd.

All this I am highlighting will lead to my next point in the next chapter which is:

An MLM That Would Suit YOU

Understanding this principle could save your MLM life. Many people label everyone who joins more than one MLM company a 'junkie'. It is true that there are junkies that goes around recruiting their friends when he tries COMPANY A, dies a natural death after a while and joins COMPANY B. He starts talking to the same friends how good COMPANY B is and always talk bad about COMPANY A. Then he quits COMPANY B after running into some struggles and joins COMPANY C, does the same thing promoting C while talking bad about A and B and goes on and on.

No. I am not teaching you to be a junkie.

I have explained in the previous chapters that even the 'best company' in the world would not be suitable for everyone. I may LOVE supplements for my health and buy it from the 'best health supplement opportunity in the world' but my passion is being on the Internet! Don't get me wrong, the supplement company would have a FANTASTIC TEAM, a SOLID COMPANY BACKGROUND, and even an UNBELIEVABLE COMPANSATION PLAN. But I prefer to sell digital products. I don't care if I don't get to meet or socialize as many people in person on my Internet MLM, I don't even care if I don't operate at an office! I am making money at my Internet MLM.

I think we get the picture now...

Here is another scenario. What do you do when you are already in one MLM and a good friend approaches you for another? Do you refuse? Remember, you must not treat your MLM business like a RELIGION. I don't refuse because I will always find benefits in every MLM company that I join. I may like the products there. I can SHARE these products (for example, supplements) to friends who do not believe in buying on the Internet! No single company will cover the ENTIRE market so we have to be realistic. I may even join that company so I can build relationships with them and get them to try my own MLM products too! If I don't keep an eye out for other opportunities, I don't feel that I am a good business man. But you must FOCUS on one business, some may say. Yes, I focus on one, but I also open the door to many other potential customers too.

Always be open to new opportunities and cross sell! That's where you put the 'network' in network marketing. But don't make the mistake of joining every opportunity just to get people because it costs you time and money and only join different MLMs if you see a tangible benefit.

If you don't make it in your first MLM, don't despair! People make mistakes and they (hopefully) grow wiser the next time they choose again. This is what I hope for all who read this book because you must never give up when you fail the first time. Most people don't make it in their first MLM but they might succeed in the second or third.

Being Aware of the Risks

In any business dealings there are always risks – Same in life. Drive out the door today and there are always risks of accidents. How to minimize your risks also depends on your own judgment.

Before joining a company, you must always remember in MLM that if you want to make serious money, you must be prepared to be in for the long haul. There are people who tell themselves, if I can make $500 to $1,000 part time/on the side, I would be happy. They do not set their goals high and what happens? They give only part time or half hearted effort which often doesn't even help them make the $500 that they wanted in the first place!

Others think to themselves, that if they can find that ONE opportunity, I'll be one of their first and look for 2-5 downlines, which will do the rest of the work (network building) then I will be set for life. MLM requires HARD WORK. MLM is a business that appreciates in value OVER TIME. Which would you rather earn?

$10,000 a day every month?

OR

$0.01 doubling every day per month?

Ten thousand a day would seem like a lot of money on the first day compared with getting one cent on the first day? Most would choose the first option, but consider.

$10,000 * 30 days is $300,000. If 31 days, then it would be $310,000

1 cent doubling every day would product a whopping $5,368,709.12!!!

If we add one more day the total will be over 10 million!!!

Don't despair if you don't make substantial money over the first 6 months. Those are your TRAINING months. Remember again, NO ONE SUCCEEDS IN THE MLM INDUSTRY WITHOUT LEARNING AND HANDS ON EXPERIENCE.

Learn to pace yourself. Rome is not built in a day. But do it at a proper pace where you know your financial limitations. Ask yourself:

- Can you afford the joining fees?
- Are you prepared for the obvious overheads like petrol, food and training materials?
- If you don't make money in the first six months, can you survive?
- Are you prepared to cut down on your luxuries so you can work out your business?
- Are you prepared to LEARN?

Getting Started Off The Right Foot

Once you have answered all the questions in the previous chapter, you begin your journey.

Attend trainings repeatedly and listen to your upline. If your upline is not qualified, the keep going upline until you find someone who can coach you or mentor you.

Once you have downlines under you, you must be prepared to be a leader and duplicate what your upline has taught you.

DUPLICATION is the key to building a long term business because your downlines are able to do the same thing you are doing. Many successful leaders in MLM are fantastic speakers on the stage and powerful trainers in the field and even write books on how to succeed. One of the biggest mistakes a new distributor usually makes are buying a ton of books thinking they will be well equipped to go 'out there' and create a sponsoring explosion. You may try to imitate your leader, talk like them, look confident or even walk like them. But the tricky part is duplicating the charisma or having the same influence. Even after reading all the books on self-improvement, the tactics might not work because you don't have the same charm as the author!

I am not saying don't read books or buy books. Factual information or education is usually more helpful in making a good decision. I have compiled a reading list at the end of this book that will give good facts. But trying to become like another person and using his or her 'techniques' will often lead to disappointment with the book itself! They become disillusioned and go on to buy another 'key to success in MLM' book and the vicious cycle repeats itself again.

Eventually they become disillusioned with books and they will stop reading all together.

KEY POINT TO REMEMBER:

Leaders are not born, they are developed over time. Those who succeed in MLM will have to pay the price of learning and growing. Those who succeed quickly in MLM has already paid the price or were lucky enough to find downlines who had already paid the price.

ARE *YOU* PREPARED TO PAY THE PRICE?

In a Nutshell

MLM is not an easy road to walk on and there will be many obstacles along the way. That is why choosing the RIGHT company is of utmost importance as the journey of a thousand miles begin with the first step so I hope everyone reading this will take the first step in the RIGHT direction.

Regardless of success or failure, MLM is a journey worth traveling on because of the things you will learn along the way. It is priceless.

It is with my sincerest wishes that all who read this book would achieve tremendous success in the MLM journey.

Resources

Get Related Materials

from Our Free Library

Instant Access – Join Here

Click or type into your browser:

http://livesensical.com/go/byob/